Needle Felting Handbook

A Beginners Guide for Crafting 9 Intricate Needle Felting Patterns and Felted Animals With Wool Plus Essential Instructions and Supplies Included

By

Zera Meyer

Copyright © 2022 – Zera Meyer

All rights reserved

No part of this publication may be reproduced, distributed, or transmitted in any form or by any means, including photocopying, recording, or other electronic or mechanical methods, without the prior written permission of the publisher, except in the case of brief quotations embodied in reviews and certain other non-commercial uses permitted by copyright law.

Disclaimer

This publication is designed to provide competent and reliable information regarding the subject matter covered. However, the views expressed in this publication are those of the author alone, and should not be taken as expert instruction or professional advice. The reader is responsible for his or her own actions.

The author hereby disclaims any responsibility or liability whatsoever that is incurred from the use or application of the contents of this publication by the purchaser or reader. The purchaser or reader is hereby responsible for his or her own actions.

Table of Contents

Introduction 6

Chapter 1 8

Needle Felting Fundamentals 8

    What is Needle Felting? 8

    The Origin of Needle Felting 9

    What You Can Make With Needle Felting 12

    Benefits of Needle Felting 13

    Making Money From Needle Felting 17

    Selling Your Needle Felted Crafts 19

Chapter 2 23

Tips and Techniques In Needle Felting 23

    Before You Start Poking 23

    Needle Felting The Main Object 25

    Adding Details to Your Object and Finishing Touches 28

Chapter 3 30

Needle Felting Tools and Supplies 30

    Needle Felting Needles 30

        Triangular needle 31
        Spiral needle 32
        Star needle 32
        Reverse needle 33
    Felting Needle Pens 35

    Needle Felting Wool 36

    Needle Felting Pad or Foam 39

    Other Supplies 40

Chapter 4 42

Needle Felting Project Patterns 42

    Owls 42

    Bees 48

    Mushroom 53

    Penguin 64

    Sheep 70

    Gnome 76

    Flower Brooch 88

    Loop Bracelet 94

    Pumpkin Earrings 105

Chapter 5 113

Fixing Common Needle Felting Problems 113

Conclusion 120

Introduction

Needle felting is a very interesting, fascinating, and inexpensive type of needlework that has gained popularity in modern times. Modern craftswomen use this technique to make clothes, toys, shoes, all kinds of accessories, and jewelry, to mention but a few.

Needle felting is not a relatively new craft but is one of the oldest types of needlework: people made objects from felted wool about 8 thousand years ago. Legend has it that the first felted carpert was created on Noah's ark. Presently, this technique is gaining more creative ideas that allow you to create amazing pieces or objects.

In its most basic form, felting is the technique of condensing and binding animal fibers together to create a dense and sturdy fabric or shape. This is usually done with wool, but it may also be done with alpaca, yak, camel, cashmere, angora, mohair, and llama protein animal fibers. Although each of these fibers comes with some characteristics that enable them to felt, some are more suited to the task than others.

To begin felting with the needle and wool, you need to be well informed and educated about the nitty-gritty of this craft. And to get off on the right note, you need a step-by-step guide to take you by the hand along the journey – this is where this book, *Needle Felting Handbook*, comes in. This book is written to arm you with the necessary knowledge resource needed (tools, supplies, tips, techniques, project ideas, etc.) to begin felting beautiful pieces of objects today.

Without much ado, let's jump right into it!

Chapter 1

Needle Felting Fundamentals

What is Needle Felting?

Needle felting is a technique that entails repeatedly piercing a piece of wool with a needle to stiffen and mold it into the desired shape. Because the texture of the felted crafts mimics an animal's fur, it's becoming a trendy method for making little animal sculptures. Food, plants, and cartoon characters are a few of the popular items that needle felters enjoy making.

A unique type of needle is utilized in manipulating wool fibers to create objects when it's continuously poked into a ball of wool. Tiny barbed notches on the needle's tip allow the wool fibers to move towards the middle of the shape without pulling out when the needle is pushed out. The more you do this, the stiffer your shape will become.

The repeated motions of the needle may be quite relaxing; therefore, needle felting is becoming a popular method of stress treatment. The nice part about needle felting is that you don't need a lot of supplies to get started.

Needle felting may seem a bit long and laborious at first, but if you get the hang of it, it becomes relatively easy to control your hand gesture to force the wool to contract in the direction you want in forming your intended object.

You don't need to be an expert in needle felting to start. In addition to being creative, this technique is very noble and different from others. All you need is to be very enthusiastic and willing to learn the tricks of the craft.

The Origin of Needle Felting

When most people hear the word "felting," they instantly think of wet felting. Felt evolved around 5000-4000 BC after sheep were domesticated for wool. Sheep were the earliest domesticated animals, and they were bred for meat, milk, and their skin. This evolved, and they were now preserved for their wool, which was used to manufacture clothing.

In the 1800s, needle felting was discovered. In 1859, the first self-evident for a needle punching machine was issued. Originally, the machines were designed to manufacture striking and padding out of soldier's haircuts, abattoir fibers, and other materials. Needle felting was used as an alternative to the traditional method of making felted fabric using soap and water.

The felting industry produced felt for a variety of applications, including carpet underlay, auto carpets, and more. The tennis ball is the most well-known product of felting. The tennis ball is covered in a felted material that possesses streamlined qualities.

David and Eleanor Stanwood, who came to Martha's Vineyard from California in the 1980s, worked with Belgian felt producers. The felt makers operated a few textile mills that still used carding equipment to prepare wool.

With the emergence of the cotton and manufactured fiber industries, the use of fleece was progressively fading into history. These ranchers didn't know what to do with their fleece. They started by turning the fleece into batts for blankets and sofas, but as an afterthought, they experimented with the instruments. Eleanor got a few felting needles gotten from the mills to produce felt, as David and Eleanor intended to make light batting for comforters and quilts. Eleanor progressed from quilts to sewing wraps and scarves with the felt technique, thus displaying her creativity.

Ayala Tapai, a textile artist from California, learned of these felting needles in some way. Ayala had received a handful of needles as well as a sample-sized needle punch machine from a friend. Ayala experimented with the machine in her kitchen, which came from an obsolete textile business.

Birgitte Krag Hansen, a Danish felt craftswoman, learned about the procedure through Ayala. Birgitte had been using the wet felting technique to create sculptural felt. She immediately recognized the potential for using this approach to create three-dimensional basic pieces.

It didn't take long for the procedure to spread throughout Scandinavia.

Trolls, pixies, and fairies were thereafter seen all over the world, and the art began to spread throughout the North Sea to the United Kingdom. Needle felting is rapidly approaching the same level of popularity as wet felting, with some outstanding examples seen in Japan.

As the globe gradually adopted this technique, certain textile artists led the way, incorporating it into their work and handing on their knowledge to others. Many of the artists had previously worked with wet felting, which was the first type of felting to be used. And that's how needle felting became popular all over the world.

What You Can Make With Needle Felting

Animals are a favorite option among needle felters, and it's easy to see why: specific felting needles provide a fuzzy appearance that resembles fur. You don't have to confine yourself to animals that are stand-alone or to other items; an item like a scarf can also serve as a base for felted objects.

Butterflies can be needle felted, likewise flowers, or other ornaments directly onto the surface with a pair of gloves. (If you're needle felting onto a hand-knit object, ensure the gauge is tight, so the felting surface is as smooth as possible.) You can also needle-felt a heart or some other shape onto a plain sweater or needle felting a fabric cuff to add some color.

Needle felting isn't simply for decoration; it may also be used for mending. Is there a hole in your beloved sweater? To repair it, use needle felting.

Benefits of Needle Felting

Let's take a look at some of the benefits of needle felting;

1. **Needle felting promotes meditation**

Needle felting is a series of small, quiet and repetitive gestures. Many see it as a kinship with meditation. Needle felting anchors in the here, slowing down breathing and soothing the heartbeat. Once you have mastered the needle felting technique, you'd discover that it's a very relaxing activity. When you make a simple piece, the stitches are always the same, helping you escape mentally. The repetitive and relaxing movement will give your body and mind the same benefits as a meditation session. Except that in addition, you will have a nice piece at the end.

2. **Needle felting reduces memory loss**

Numerous studies have linked needle felting to a reduction in memory problems. This craft provides a soothing feel for those with dementia, but it also triggers memories and decreases anxiety, all of which help to delay memory loss.

3. Needle felting improves self-esteem

Engaging in a needle felting activity allows you to take up challenges by starting with small, simple projects and gradually taking up elaborate projects. Getting to make something with your hands is always rewarding, especially when it took hours of work to make. We can only feel proud when we see the end result or when people inquire about its origin. This exciting feeling helps build your self-confidence and also reflects in different aspects of your life.

4. It's cheap to start

Needle felting supplies are not really pricey as other similar crafts. To begin needle felting, all you'll need is a needle (or several needles, as they're easy to break when you're learning), wool roving, and a sponge or foam block to act as your "work surface." The needle is very fragile and can break if it comes into contact with a hard surface such as a table top; hence, the foam/sponge block is required. Your needle will be protected if you place your work on top of the foam block. For about $9.99, you can purchase a complete kit of essential supplies (and a few more things that will make felting faster) from Amazon or your local craft store.

Wool roving is also reasonably priced; you can generally acquire a variety of distinct colors of wool roving for $10 to $15, which will last you for a long time. The cost isn't nearly as high as the supplies required to begin knitting or crocheting.

5. Spend less and earn more

Needle felting can even become more than a hobby because you can spend less to purchase the required supplies, and if you are creative enough and learn to felt quickly, you can sell your creations or felt in exchange for a few bucks.

It can be a great way to make ends meet; make some pocket money if you're a student, or start your own business.

6. It's easy to learn compared to other crafts

Needless to say, "easy" is a subjective term, but if you find the various procedures in knitting or crocheting to be onerous, you'll be relieved to learn that needle felting isn't quite as demanding. Basically, if you can repeatedly stab a clump of wool with a needle, you can needle felt. There's no need to memorize loops or stitches! If you don't want to, you don't need to follow patterns. The only challenging aspect of needle felting is that it takes a long time. A tiny, easy needle felting creation can take up to two hours to complete, while more elaborate pieces might take days to weeks to complete.

However, rather than use a single needle, you can accelerate the process with the use of a felting pen, which accommodates three needles. It's also a very tolerant medium, making it difficult to make a mistake. Because it takes a lot of needle pokes to permanently shape or indent the wool, it's quite easy to spot faults before they become permanent. If you don't like the way it looks, you can simply "massage" it with your hand to correct any dents or just add more wool to hide imperfections.

7. You can create any project

With needle felting, the possibilities are endless. Though it is labeled as "fiber arts," I believe it is more akin to clay sculpting. You can make anything you can imagine. Some people make little miniatures of people or animals, while others create large models and abstract art. You have complete creative control.

Making Money From Needle Felting

Needle felting is a fun and relaxing hobby that can be turned into a money-making venture. Earning money doing something you like is wonderful because you enjoy the activity you do and receive financial reward in return.

Here are some ideas that can help you earn with needle felting;

1. **Sell your pieces**

Take good photos of your felted work and upload them to different marketplaces. It would help if you got your friends and family to buy your crafts and to refer others to you; the power of referrals can create wonders.

2. **Work based on commission**

You can receive commissioned work instead of making a lot of items. This way, you'll know you will sell the item and won't waste time on items that won't sell or won't sell for a long time. It's a good idea to have a contract and a payment in this situation.

3. **Make and sell your own kits**

This is quite well-liked. If you can create and sell needle felting kits, you'll be able to expand your business.

4. **Provide lessons online**

This is an option, but there are many free ones available online, so doing free ones to develop trust may be more useful at first, then gradually transition to paid services.

5. **Make books and sell**

You can choose to make money by selling your crafts in the form of a book. Books can be sold in needle felting communities, craft fairs, specialized Facebook groups, on marketplaces like Amazon.

6. **Provide lessons offline**

You can design and administer lessons in your local area, and you'll also be able to sell your needle felting kits, books, and equipment to your students while at it.

Selling Your Needle Felted Crafts

You need to make your crafts known to attract the needed traffic to make money, and there is no other way other than advertising your needle-felted crafts through offline and online channels. As you know, these places are more profitable and easier to get interested buyers. So, let's take a look at some of the available mediums through which you can sell;

1. **Etsy**

This appears to be the best place to go if you want to sell any of your handmade items online, whether it's needle felting or something else. Etsy will be the starting point for most craftspeople.

Although you can sell products on Etsy without any extra support system, I believe that it will hinder your sales. This is due to the large number of people selling various items on Etsy. So there's a slim probability that someone will discover your work. You must also advertise yourself outside of Etsy in order to get consumers to sell your things on Etsy.

You'll also need a few other things, which I've listed below.

2. Facebook

Facebook is a popular platform for crafters to sell their services. They frequently share their works or services in groups and on their personal profile pages. Recently, I heard from some bloggers (not crafting bloggers) that Facebook is clamping down on businesses and has not become much of a good place to sell your crafts.

3. Amazon

If you are selling your own kit or even wool, you might want to look into Amazon or eBay, as well as Etsy and Facebook.

4. Craft fairs

These events take place even in small towns. To be useful to your business, it is important to study the reviews of experienced crafts people who have gone there before. You have to pay for the opportunity to present your products at the fairs, so participation is not always economically profitable - earnings may not cover the costs. To make money, you need to sell products in a specific season.

Craft fairs are a good way to have your name out there, in my opinion. It's more about establishing your brand and becoming well-known. Giving your business cards to people is also a priority. So it's worth thinking about.

5. Local craft shops or marketplaces

If you have a nearby location where you may sell your things, it can be worthwhile to do so. Some people have had success with this, while others have experienced challenges. Not every store will look after your items. This would be on the basis of a sale or a return.

6. Your own website

Creating your own website and e-commerce to sell your crafts is a smart way to go.

Having your own website is vital. Not these free setups, but your own website using WordPress and a domain name. These days, they are easy to set up, and anyone can do it with little practice. The purpose for having your own website is because you are advertising yourself and your services, and in order to do so, you'll need your own internet real estate. It's also not a good idea to rely solely on other businesses to market your work because it's all too usual for them to fail or change their policies.

Chapter 2

Tips and Techniques In Needle Felting

Before You Start Poking

1. If you'd be crafting a small piece, start off by rubbing the wool in-between your hands to make a ball. This will enable the fibers to tangle a little to provide an easier felting process.
2. For medium and bigger pieces, keeping the wool in a smooth sheet would be a better idea so that you wouldn't have to smooth out bumps. However, if you cannot decide the amount of wool needed, your best shot would be to start with a smaller piece, then have some extra wool wrapped around it to make it bigger.
3. It's possible to have larger felted pieces filled with polyfill or acrylic stuffing to save on wool. All you have to do is start by felting acrylic stuffing into a solid mass before having it covered up with wool. Alternatively, you can have the sewing thread rolled around the polyfill before covering it up with felting wool. If your next piece is most

likely round and large, then this is a technique to consider.
4. It's no longer news that needles are delicate and are prone to breaking easily. Ensure to have extra needles kept aside should your needle break mistakenly when working on a project.
5. Before starting a new project, always keep a small amount of wool in different colors. This is a great idea if you need to make corrections or slight modifications to your project, thereby giving your work an almost perfect look upon completion.
6. If your project has a triangular, circular, or heart-like shape, using a cookie cutter or stencil would be a nice idea to have your piece shaped out accordingly.

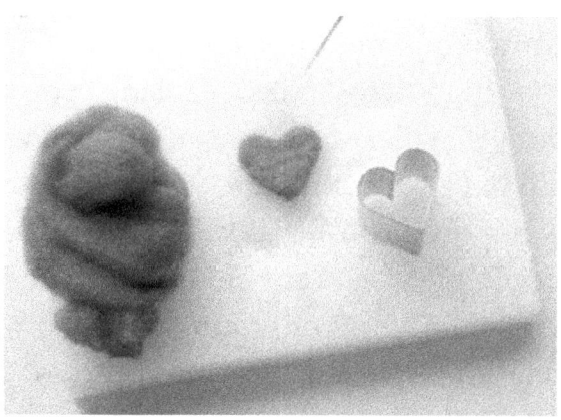

Needle Felting The Main Object

7. Start by stuffing the stencil with wool in the previous step, place it on your mat and start poking away. Flip your stencil (with the wool inside) over, poking its other side. Continue poking and turning your piece until it is hard and takes the form of your stencil. After that, work on firming up the edges and fine-tuning your work.
8. To prevent yourself from being poked, hold the wool so that you can view your fingers, then poke slowly and carefully.
9. When you start poking, it's normal for the wool to be fluffy and soft. However, as you progress with the stabs, you'll notice the wool gradually taking shape and getting denser like a cotton ball. A continuous poking of the wool would further create more crosslinks, causing your wool to become smaller and denser; this takes time, so you'll have to be patient.
10. The importance of a needle felting pen (where multiple needles can be used at once to felt) cannot be under-emphasized as it can dramatically speed up the process of needle felting.

11. To prevent the needle from breaking, always take it out in the same direction it went in. Poke the needle straight up and down, not tilting it while inside the wool.

    Also, forcing a needle into wool can only lead to breakage. When your felted object becomes difficult to penetrate, it's advisable to poke in the needle slowly and carefully to avoid breakage.

12. When you want to create a circular, uniform ball, your best shot would be to evenly poke around your piece without focusing on just one spot except for specific shapes you want your wool molded into.
13. When connecting small pieces, create some fluffy felt at the edge of the smaller piece where you intend attaching it to the bigger piece. Create a hole with your needle in the bigger piece where the smaller piece will enter, or make a small opening with scissors in the bigger piece, stuffing your smaller piece tip inside. Then sew the two pieces together with your needle.

Tip: When making small pieces that need to be attached to the main body, leave one end fluffy.

14. When attaching black plastic eyes, use your needle to make a mark on the spot where you intend to place the eyes before proceeding to create holes with either an awl or scissors. If you don't mind, add a little bit of glue to eye's end before sticking them in the holes.
15. If your needle breaks and becomes stuck in your felted object, squeeze lightly to reveal the broken needle. When squeezing, however, take caution not to put your fingers in the location where the needle's pointed end is positioned. Pull the broken needle out with tweezers, calmly but firmly. Or, try cutting your felted object with scissors in the location where the needle dropped and search for it. After you've pulled out the

needle, reassemble your object using bits of loose wool.

Adding Details to Your Object and Finishing Touches

16. If you felt a piece of wool with a different color on an existing felted object, do not felt it down too firmly because the underlying object's shape might be altered, and the freshly felted wool piece will be lost in the larger one. Use your needle to carefully poke the wool fibers into the main object to keep it in place.
17. If your final project has any unpleasant gaps, take a small piece of the same colored wool, wrap it into a ball, and slowly use your needle to felt it gently into the gap. Felt until it is completely absorbed into the final piece, closing the gap.
18. Don't be hesitant to use your needle to pick off the top bits of wool if you're unhappy with the finishing touches of your work. Then, to fill in any holes in the main body of your work, add a bit of felting wool and recreate the touches.
19. Using too much wool while making small facial details is a common mistake. Often, all you need is a pretty small strand of wool for eyes, noses, and mouths. Keep in mind that adding

extra definition later on is easier than it is to completely remove the piece and start over.
20. Sew a mouth or whiskers with embroidery thread and a needle. This method is more consistent and neater than felting on a tiny strand of wool.
21. For childlike pieces, you can use wool to stand in for the eyes rather than opting for the black plastic eyes in kits or that is gotten separately.
22. Melamine foam should not be used in your projects because it is highly hazardous if ingested.
23. Gently poke the surface of your piece when rounding up to tuck in loose fibers before trimming off excesses with scissors to smoothen the project well enough.

Chapter 3

Needle Felting Tools and Supplies

This craft does not take a lot of supplies to start. A needle, some wool, and a piece of foam are all you'll need in most cases.

Let's take a look at the tools and supplies needed to complete your needle felting pieces;

Needle Felting Needles

Needle felting necessitates the use of a special needle with pointed tips. The fibers can be drawn into the middle of the wool with these points, resulting in a hard felt. The further you poke the wool fiber with a needle, the harder the fibers get.

Modest "fast" movements are necessary with the needle. There is no need to completely insert the needle inside the wool to stir up the fiber. It's also important to pull out the needle in the same direction it was first inserted to avoid damaging it. Don't push a needle into the wool if it seems too stiff. Finish or proceed to a new location with a lower gauge needle.

Types of Felting Needles

Spiral, star, triangular, and reverse felting needles are the four varieties of felting needles. These are generally distinguished by the needle's cross-section shape, but they also have additional qualities that set them apart:

Triangular needle

This type of needle is generally used in needle felting and easy to find, as it is ideal for most project. Three edges and a straight shaft with evenly spaced barbs characterize triangular needles.

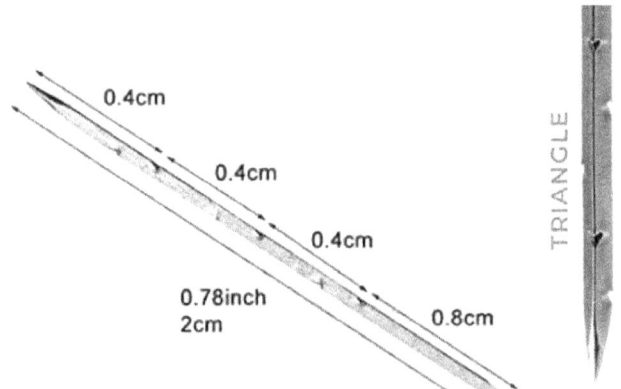

Spiral needle

Spiral (twisted) felting needles are similar to triangular needles but with a twisted blade. The spiral design allows for speedier felting due to lower penetration tension. The twisted needles bind fibers together fast, making them ideal for finishing surfaces.

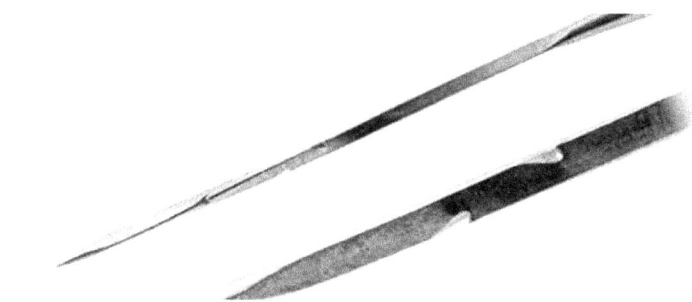

Star needle

Star felting needles feature four sides, each with two or three barbs; resulting in more barbs for faster felting. They are better suited to working with coarse fibers and are excellent for sculpting and attaching pieces together.

Reverse needle

Barbs on reverse felting needles are cut in the reverse direction as those on the other felting needles. This enables the needle to push out fibers rather than push them in. These needles can be used to create textures such as fur or fuzz, among other things. They are also used to pull inside layers of various colors to the surface and are generally ideal for creating details on your pieces

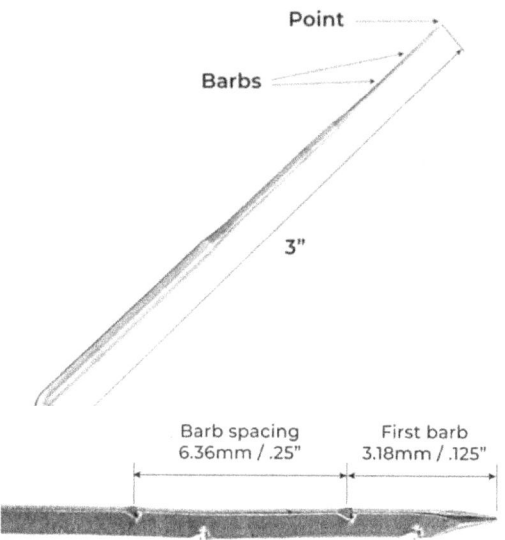

Needle Gauges

Felting needles come in sizes of 32, 36, 38, 40, and 42. If the needle size is high, then the needle itself is a thin needle. For example, a 32 gauge needle is thicker than a 36, 38, 40 or 42 gauge needle. For coarse wool, use thicker needles, whereas for thinner or finer fibers, use smaller gauges. When the wool gets too thick, use a thinner gauged needle.

If you have numerous needles, it may be difficult to distinguish which one is which, so color-code them if necessary. At the handle, I recommend putting nail paint or a little strip of colored washi tape.

Felting Needle Pens

Pens (such as the one below) could also assist in improving the needle felting process. This pen can accommodate up to three needles at once, making felting more productive. It also has a more robust grip, making it easier to control.

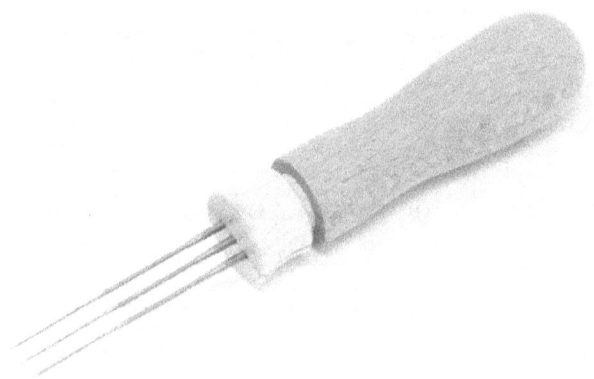

What is the best needle for needle felting?

Generally, you should have a selection of needle types in various gauges. Several needles may be included in certain kits. You may also buy needle packs for a reasonable price, as you'll almost certainly break some of them eventually. If that isn't possible, a 38-gauge needle would be an excellent choice for a beginner. The type of needle you use depends on your preference, but a spiral or triangular needle is the ideal place to start.

Needles are also made with different numbers of notches. Although having a bigger number of grooves might help you to felt more productively, it may not be required when making more complex work. Keep this in mind while you shop for needles.

Needle Felting Wool

There are many different sorts of fibers from which to choose for your projects. Animal, plant, and synthetic fibers can all be used in this craft, but most felters utilize sheep's wool. Because different types of sheep yield wool with different properties, you may need to try a few to determine which you like the most - Corriedale, Merino, New Zealand, Norwegian Lincoln, Romney, Drysdale, and a variety of other breeds are among them.

Wool is often categorized in microns, in which the greater the micron, the coarser the fibers are. The roughness of the fiber is not the only consideration to factor when choosing your wool, but the way it is prepared can also influence your decision.

Wool Roving vs. Wool Batts

The two most common types of wool are roving and batts.

Wool that has been combed with specific padding (also known as carding) until all the fibers move in the same direction is known as roving. It's ideal for spinning.

Batts are thick wool sheets that have not been entirely carded, resulting in kinks of fibers that run in different directions.

Because you'll be manipulating the fiber kinks with the needle anyways, wool roving and batts are suitable for needle felting. Batts, on the other hand, may be easier to work with because the fibers already run in various different directions in a wild manner.

Best wool for needle felting

Needle felting is not suitable for all types of wool. Some wools are wonderful for wet felting (such as Merino wool), but they may not be the greatest for this craft. Fine wool has a softer, silkier feel, but coarser wool is preferable for needle felting because the needle's notches capture the scales on the fiber more easily. You'll be able to manipulate the wool more effectively as a result of this.

You'll want to use a medium-coarse fiber for needle felting. You want wool that is great to hang on to with the needle while still having a smooth finish.

1. Merino wool: Merino wool is soft and silky, and its fibers tend to be organized in the same direction, so it can be somewhat complicated to work at the beginning if you want to make needle felting pieces, but it is the best that exists for wet techniques, being the one that provides the smoother and more homogeneous finish.
2. Lana Corriedale: Corriedale wool is very good for needle felting because it is medium-coarse from 25 to 35 microns. Corriedale wool is soft, and the fibers felt very well; this means that you can work better and faster than with Merino wool or other lighter varieties.
3. New Zealand wool: This is the coarsest wool with more than 30 microns. It is excellent for needle

felting but has a rougher finish than other wools such as Merino.
4. Lana from Leicester: Of English origin, it has a thickness of 25 microns, and it is ideal for wet felting since, like merino wool, it is very fine and requires a lot of practice, although it is ideal for details and when you want to create something very focused and precise.
5. Norwegian wool: This is a medium-coarse wool well suited for needle felting and more coarse than Merino and Corriedale.

Needle Felting Pad or Foam

To keep your project grounded as you work on it, use a needle felting pad or foam. It also prevents needle damage to surfaces (and your fingers). Coarse brush is preferred by some felters. It's better to use a thick, solid piece of foam. You don't have to buy one because you can make one with items you already have around the house.

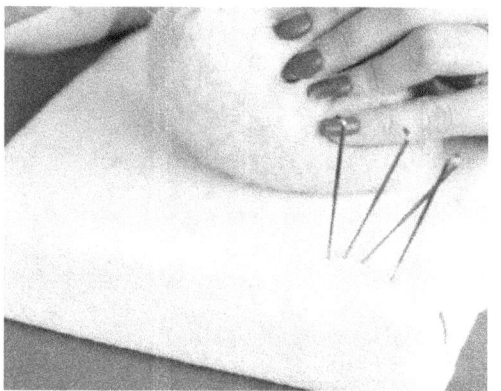

Other Supplies

As you gain experience, you'll discover additional tools and supplies that suit your demands. Finger guards or protectors, on the other hand, may be useful for beginners who don't want to stab their fingers as they needle felt. Even if you take it slowly and carefully, you'll almost certainly poke yourself.

A Short Message From The Author:

Hey, I hope you are enjoying the book? I would love to hear your thoughts!

Many readers do not know how hard reviews are to come by and how much they help an author.

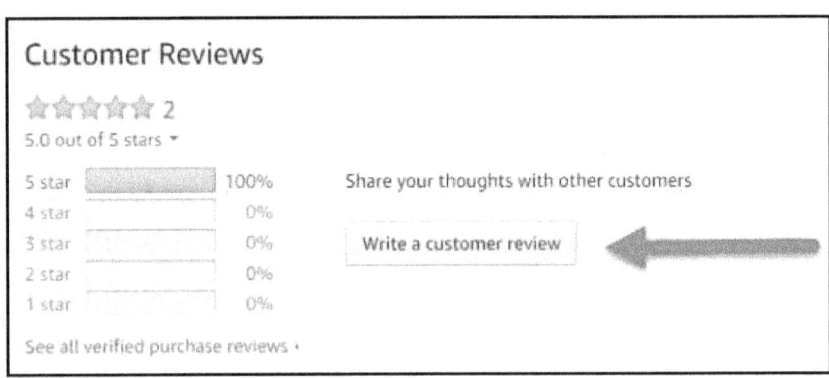

I would be incredibly grateful if you could take just 60 seconds to write a short review on Amazon, even if it is a few sentences!

\>\> Click here to leave a quick review

Thanks for the time taken to share your thoughts!

Chapter 4

Needle Felting Project Patterns

Having discussed practically most of what you need to get started in molding needle felted pieces, its now time to focus on needle felting projects you can take on as a first timer while making room for your own creativiy and ingenunity.

Owls

Tools and Supplies

- Wool roving (white, brown and a bit of tan)
- Brown string of wool roving
- Needle felting needle
- Needle felting foam board or pad

Instructions

1. To make your owl's body, start by cutting off a piece of white wool roving. It should be of the same length, width, and thickness as your hand.

2. As if you were shaping a ball of playdough into a snake, rub the white wool roving in-between your palms.

3. Begin from the short end in rolling the wool 'snake' into a dense spiral.

4. Poke your needle gently into the wool on the spiral's outside. This will ensure that your spiral maintains its shape even if you let go.

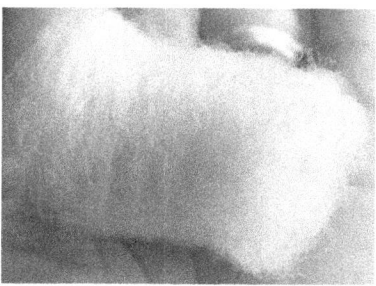

5. Poke your felting needle inside the wool to round the spiral's upper end. This will be the head of your owl.

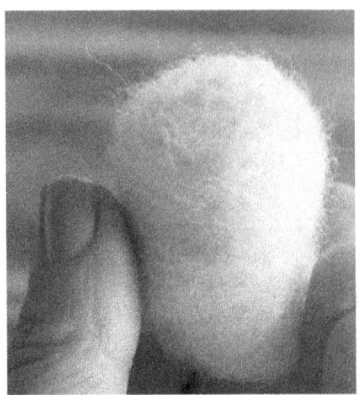

6. With your needle, flatten your spiral's bottom end. Carry on until the body of your owl can stand by itself.

7. Now for your owl's face. Cut two lengths of brown wool string that are roughly the same length and thickness as your needle. Rub the

string in-between your palms to make each piece neat and tight.

8. Felt the wool string with your needle inside the face of your owl in a heart's shape. You should have something like this.

9. Pinch a tiny quantity of brown wool roving and roll into a ball of two to form the eyes.

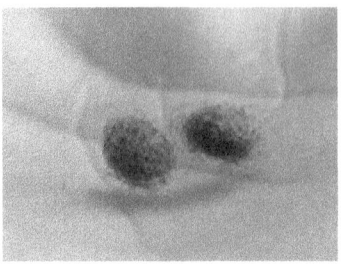

10. Pinch a tiny quantity of tan wool, rolling it into a ball to form the owl's beak.

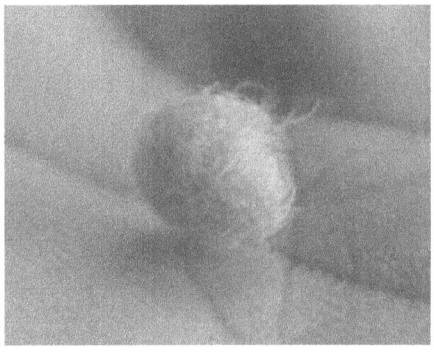

11. Felt the eyes and beak into place with your needle. Pull out a few pieces of eye wool with your needle to shape them into 'tear' forms.

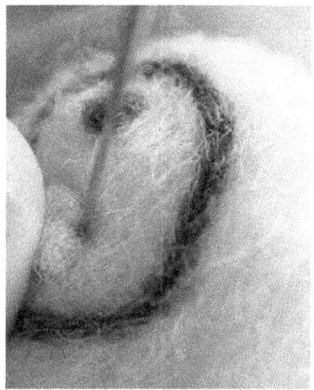

Now, we've got a very easy Barn Owl completed.

Bees

Tools and Supplies

- Wool roving (white, black, and yellow)
- Needle felting needle

- Needle felting foam board or pad

Instructions

1. To make an elongated ball, knot a 3 to 4 inch length of yellow wool and then wrap the leftover around the knot.

    Poke the ball with the felting needle until the stray bits of wool are held in place.

    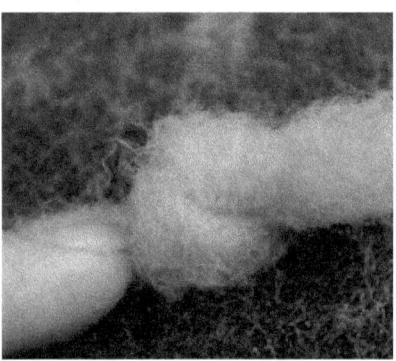

2. Take a few little wisps of black wool, rolling them into thin strands to make two 3- 4 inch lengths for the bee's stripes.

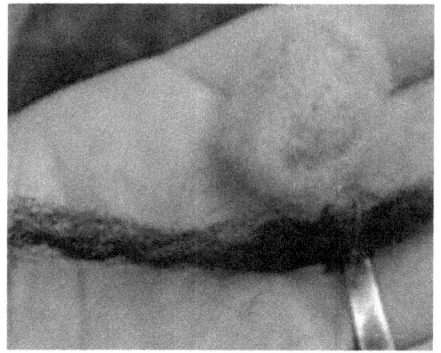

3. Wrap all over the yellow bee ball with the stripes and hold them in place with your needle.

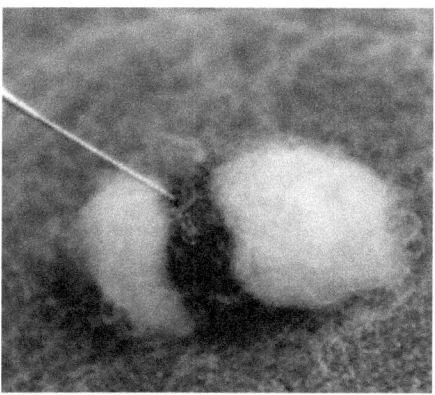

4. To make the bee's face, roll another wisp of black wool into a little ball.

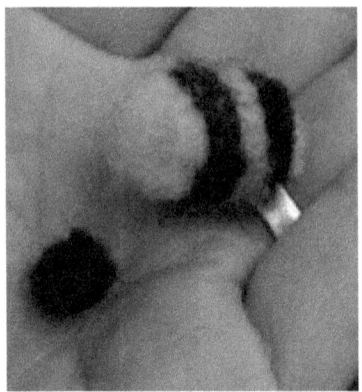

5. Needle the ball until one of the bee's end is flattened.

6. Press a thick quarter-sized piece of white wool into a wing shape with your hand's warm heels, before placing it on the felting pad.

Needle the wings on the pad until they are somewhat flat. The wool will be a little glued to the pad. Rip it up gently, flip over and needle the other side.

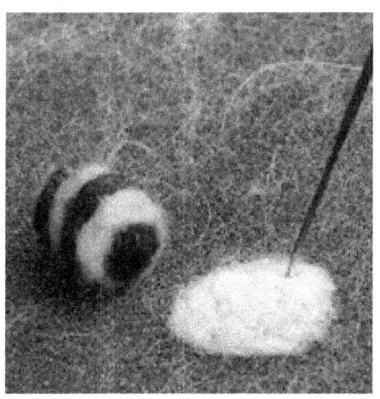

7. After being glued to the pad, the wings will be a little hazy. Carefully poke the wings onto the bee with your needle. (I worked from below, sculpting the angle so that the front side of the wings was reasonably close together than the back).

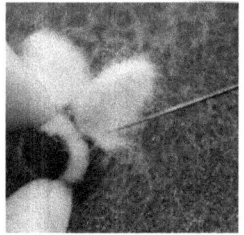

8. I needled on little eyeballs to make the little insect more lifelike.

There you go, we are done!

Mushroom

Tools and Supplies

- Wool roving (white, brown, and green)
- Needle felting needle
- Needle felting foam board or pad

Additional Supplies

- Acorn top
- Hot glue gun

Instructions

Making the stalk

1. Gather a small amount of white roving about 6 inches long, thick-as-your-thumb.

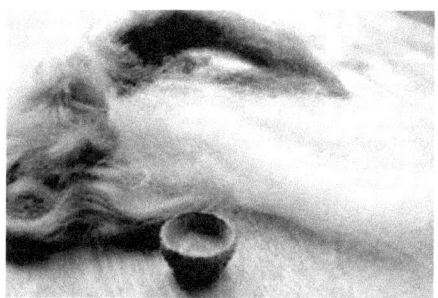

2. Gently separate the roving layers and put them on each other.

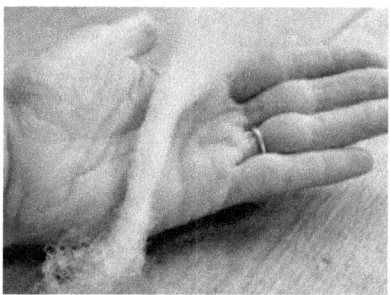

3. Roll the roving layers; the roving will begin to felt together into the shape of a stalk.

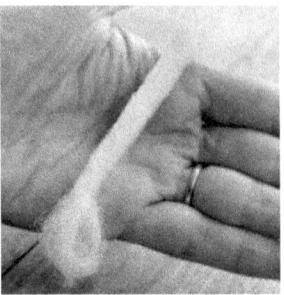

4. Using your needle, stab the roving with the stalk on the foam. The roving comes together when you stab it. Stab the stalk up and down, then turn it over, stabbing a little more. Continue in this manner until the stalk has solidified.

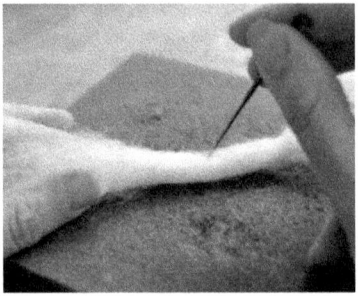

5. Allow the ends to be frayed and raw.

Making the mushroom top

6. Get some brown roving that's about 12 inches long and 2 fingers thick.

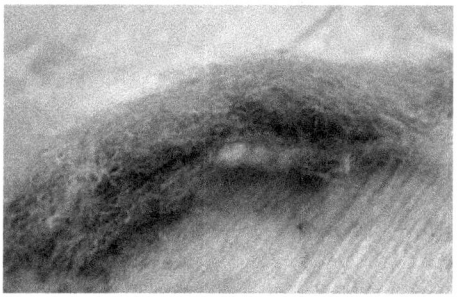

7. Make a loose coil out of the roving. Place the roving on top of the foam. Begin stabbing the needle into the roving on the outside of the coil and work your way around the roving. Pay close attention to the roving's 'seams,' which is the meeting point of two pieces.

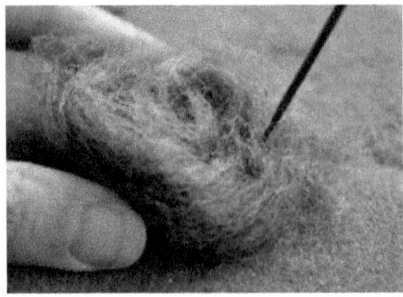

8. Grab the roving from the foam, turn it over, and felt again.

9. After the roving has felted and looks like fiber, use your fingers to carefully guide it into the desired bowl shape.

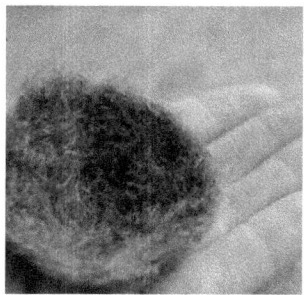

Attaching the Mushroom

10. Fray the stalk's end and gently lay the frayed end of the stalk on the cap of the mushroom. Set the two pieces (stalk and cap) on the foam and carefully poke the stalk's frayed end into the top.

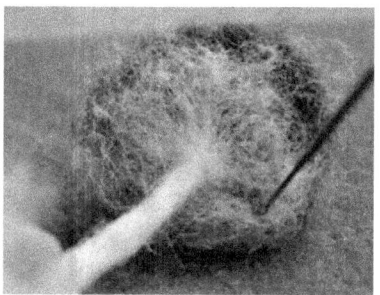

11. After the stalk frayed ends have been secured to the top of the mushroom, poke the stalk in the center, pushing it into the mushroom. Keep stabbing the stalk and the top together until they are securely connected.

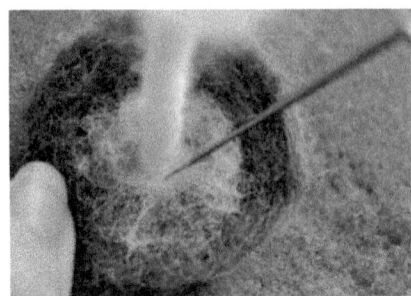

12. The stalk's white roving will be visible from the mushroom's top.

13. Coil up a little piece of brown roving to form a circle.

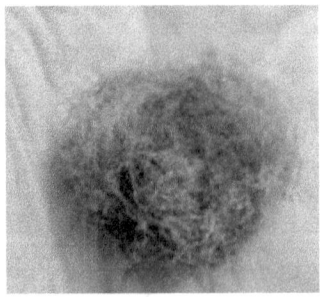

14. Felt the brown roving's small piece onto the mushroom's top, creating a small cap that will hide any visible white roving.

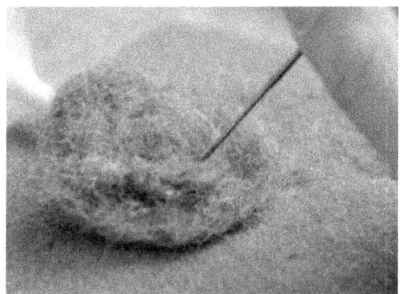 

Finishing the mushroom

15. Cut out a 6 inches long green roving, thick as your small finger. I prefer using various shades of green, but if you only want to use one, that's OK too.

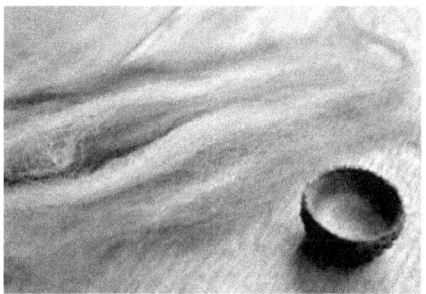

16. Separate the roving away from each other and lay them over one other. As with the mushroom top, coil the roving into a circle.

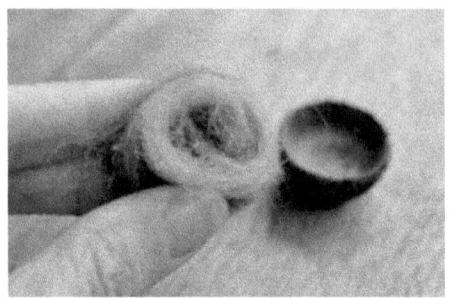

17. Felt the green roving together.

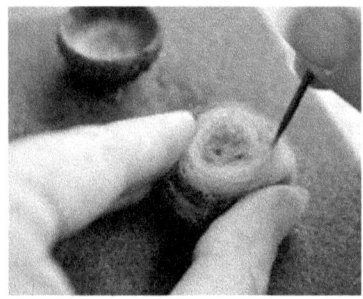

18. Use brown roving to repeat step 15. Attach the felted green piece over the felted brown piece by stabbing the two felt pieces. Pick up the pieces from the foam and move them around.

19. Attach and poke the stalk's frayed end on the green roving piece. Poke the center of the stalk, pushing into the green roving as soon as the stalk's frayed ends are joined to the green bottom. Keep poking the stalk and bottom together until they are joined well enough.

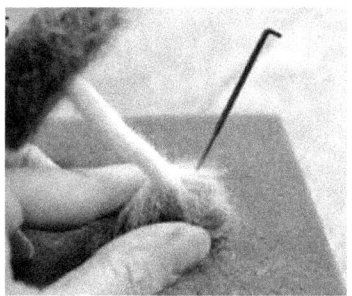

20. Wrap a strand of extra green roving around the stalk.

21. Add some tiny coils of roving for flowers if desired. Mount the mushroom on the acorn top with a hot glue gun.

You are done!

Penguin

Tools and Supplies

- Wool roving (less than 1 ounce of white wool and bits of black, gray, and orange)
- Neelde felting needle
- Needle felting foam or pad

Instructions

1. Make the body and the head

Take out a significant amount of white roving; use a felting needle to poke the wool roving all over, shaping it with your fingers as you go, until you get a thick, hard, body-shaped piece (that is about 2" long). To create a head-shaped piece, repeat with some white roving.

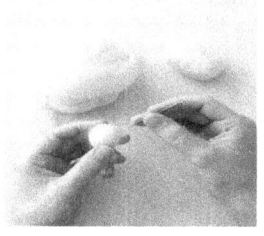

2. Adding the plumage

Take out some black wool roving and use the needle to attach it to the head. With the needle, poke the black fibers into the white so that they join, twisting the black roving into the appropriate form as you go.

3. Connect the head and the body

Use your needle to felt the head onto the body, poking the fibers with the needle and joining the two with a little extra roving, if needed.

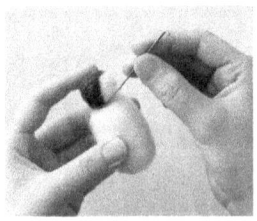

4. Make the beak, feet, wings, and eyes

To make the beak, cut out some orange roving and set it on a needle-felting pad. With the needle, poke the fibers all over the roving, pushing it into the shape of a beak as you go. Set the beak to the side.

To make two feet, repeat the beak technique with gray roving.

To make two wings, repeat with white roving.

For the eyes, cut out two little pieces of black roving. Using a needle, attach them to the top of the head. In the same way, attach the beak.

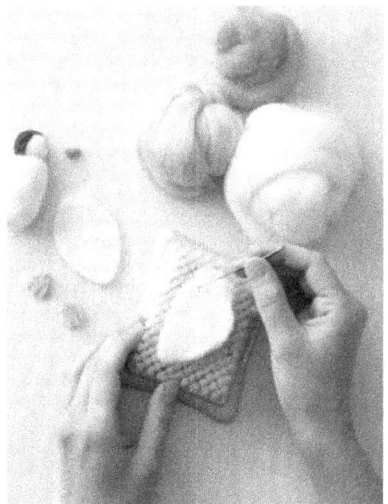

5. Add a second layer

A pocked surface on a huge needle-felted object is possible. Use your needle to felt a small layer of white roving onto the body to smooth it out and make it dense but soft.

6. Attach the wings and feet to the body

By poking with the needle, you can attach a wing to the body. Proceed with the other wing and then the feet.

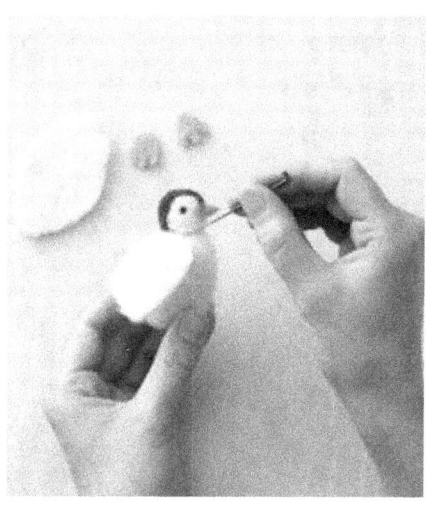

7. Make a neck

Wrap a strand of gray roving around the neck region and lightly beat it. Stop when your neck feels dense; the extra roving should be fluffy.

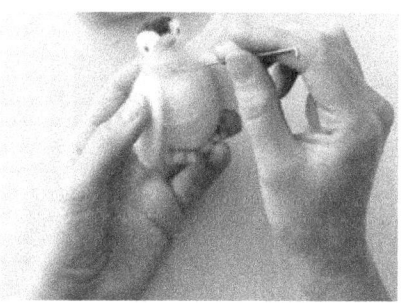

8. Make a finished appearance

Apply a small amount of gray roving around the body, lightly pressing it in place with the needle while keeping it soft and fluffy.

Sheep

Tools and Supplies

- Wool roving (white and bits of black)
- Neelde felting needle
- Needle felting foam or pad

Additional Supplies

- Foam ball or egg
- Pipe cleaners
- Embroidery floss or yarn
- Embroidery thread
- Hot glue

Instructions

1. Compress the foam ball or egg into the sheep's body shape.

2. Use your needle to felt some pieces of white wool roving onto the ball for the sheep's body.

3. Cut out some pieces of white roving wool and needle felt to form the head and ears.

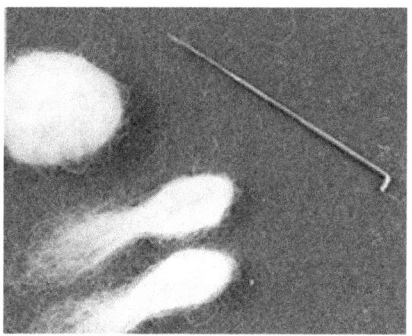

4. Join the head to the body of the sheep in step 2 using your needle. Also, wrap an additional white wool roving around the neck, blending the head to the sheep's body.

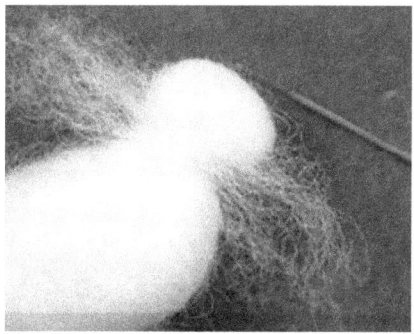

5. Use your needle to felt the ears to the sheep's head

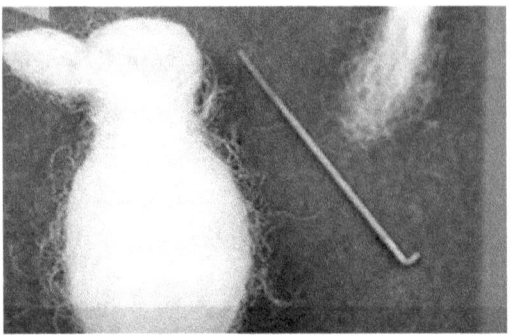

6. Cut out some pieces of white roving and use pipe cleaners to form four legs to be attached to the body with hot glue and with your felting needle.

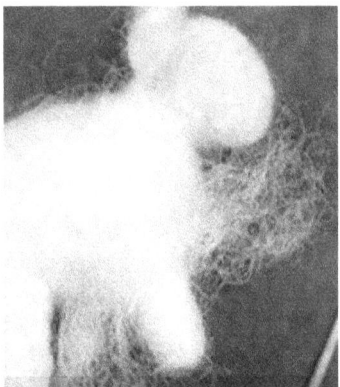

7. Smoothen out the sheep and get it into the right shape by poking loose strands of wool.

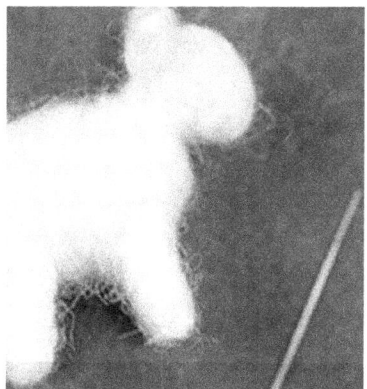

8. Make a french type of knot for the eyes using the embroidery floss, or preferably, use the black wool roving and felting needle for this.

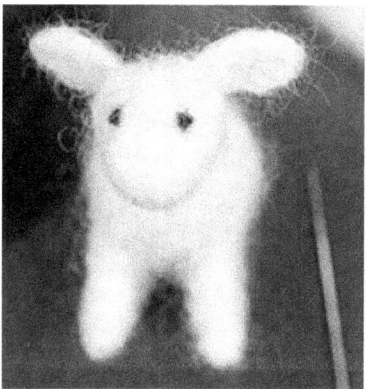

9. Make the nose and mouth of the sheep using the black roving and embroidery thread.

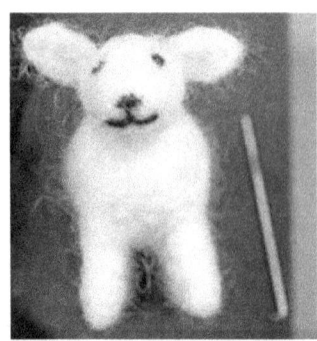

10. To shape the sheep into a fluffy form, simply twist the roving, giving you a loose fiber, then use your felting needle to needle the ends in the sheep's back.

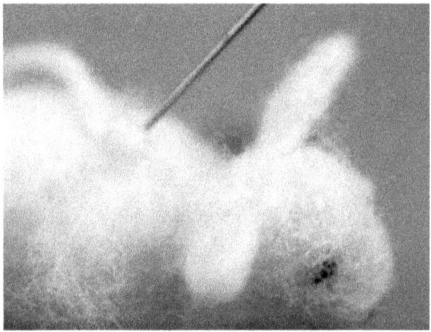

11. Keep looping the entire body of the sheep's fiber

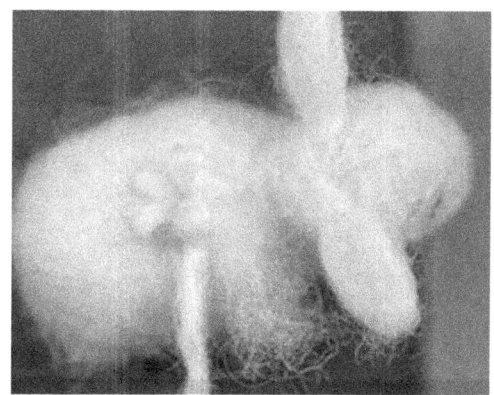

And you are done!

Gnome

Tools and Supplies

- Wool roving (for the body - blue, head – light brown, nose – light brown, hat – dark tan, and beard - white)

- Felting foam or pad
- Needle felting needle (40 gauge is preferable)

Instructions

1. Making the body

- Take out some blue colored roving for the body.
- Spin it a few times over your index finger. Note that the body will be shorter and smaller after felting than it really is over your finger.

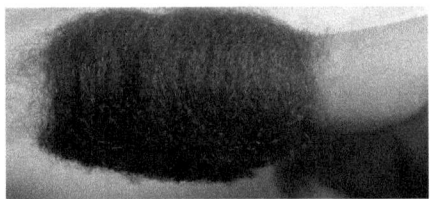

- Lay it on your felting pad after removing it from your finger.
- Turn it while poking at it. We're not attempting to change the shape at this point; instead, we're just trying to secure all of the wool so it doesn't break apart or unroll easily. You're ready to go on to the following step after removing your piece from the pad without any loose pieces hanging out.

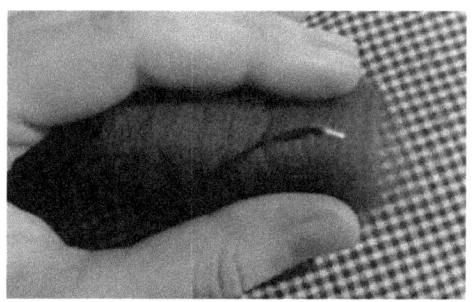

- Grab some roving with your needle, poking it down on the other side to felt the top and bottom. Basically, you want to fold a small portion of each side over to create a good base.

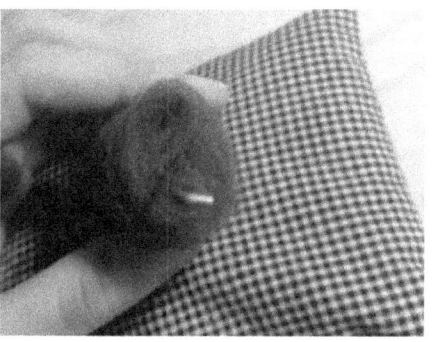

- Continue to poke at it until you achieve the desired shape and firmness. Remember that you can stab with one hand while holding the roving in the desired shape with the other hand.

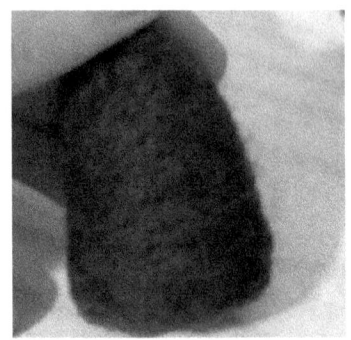

2. Making the head

- Take a handful of your light-toned brown roving. It will be slightly less than what you used for the body.

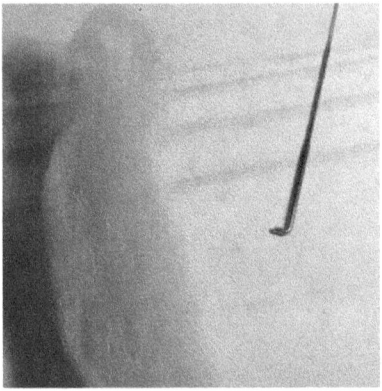

- Wrap it over your finger to produce a rough shape.

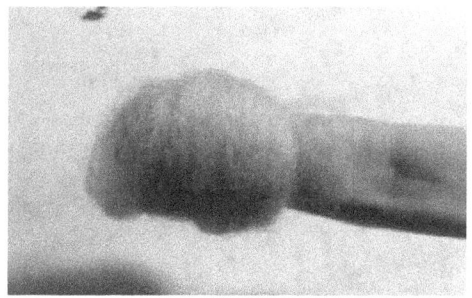

- Remove it from your finger and stab it on your felting pad while twisting it around.
- Continue stabbing until you get the desired form and size.

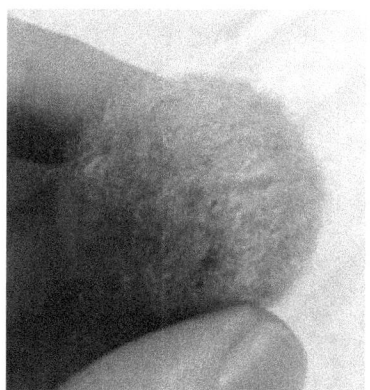

3. **Making the hat**

- Grab some dark tan roving for the cap, it will be around the same amount you used for the body.

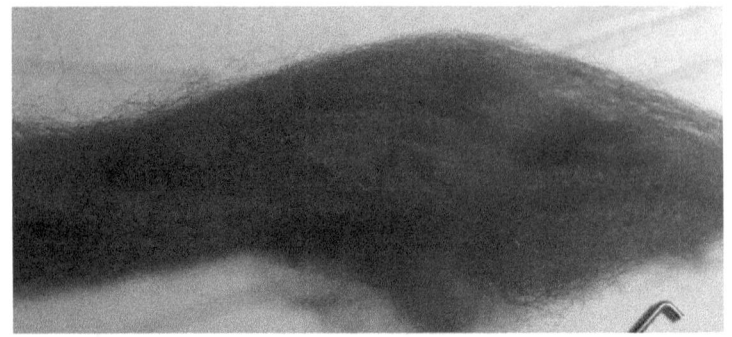

- To keep it from unrolling, wrap it over your finger and stab it on the pad.
- Make a point with one end by pinching it between your fingers. While you hold it in that place, stab the roving to maintain it in that shape .

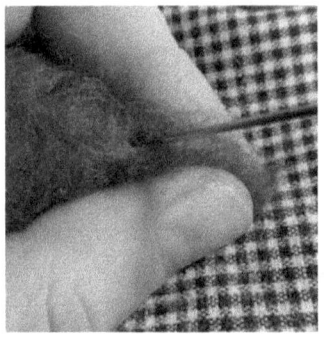

- Stab it till it's the right form and size

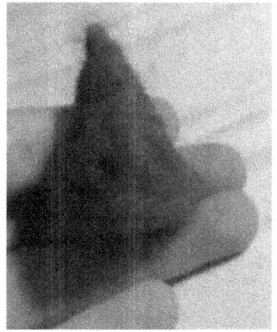

4. **Attaching the head to the body**

- Place the head above the body.
- Diagonally point your needle over the body's top and into the head, gathering part of the wool in the process.

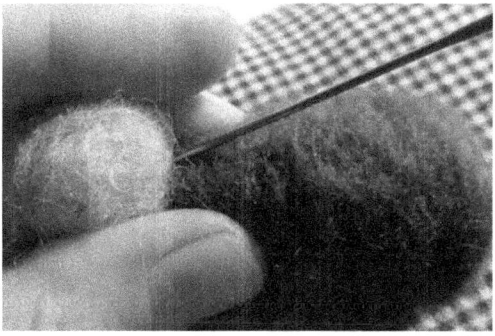

- To secure the head, felt around it.
- Now work your way down to the bottom of the body from the head's top. Because we are not

attempting to form the head, only tangle the fibers of the head with the body fibers, no need bringing your needle back out. When you're doing this, consider the location of the barbs on the needle and ensure they go deep enough into the body.

- Continue stabbing until the head is firmly connected.

5. **Attaching the hat to the head**

- Place the hat on the body in the desired location.

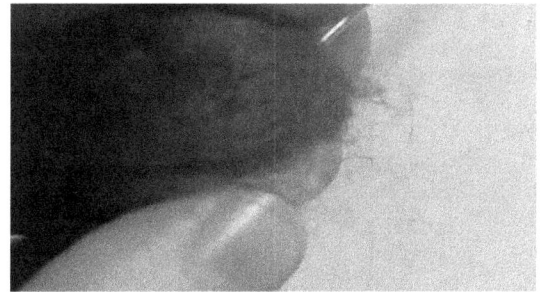

- To attach the hat, wrap felt around the rim.

6. **Adding the nose**

- Take a little amount of light brown roving.
- Form it into a ball by rolling it between your palms.

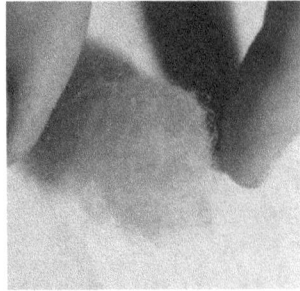

- Make a smooth ball out of it by stabbing

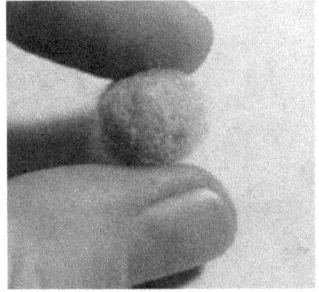

- Stab it on the head as shown below

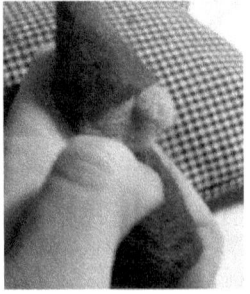

7. Fixing spaces behind the head

- If there's any space at the back of the hat where the head can be seen, cover it with hair-colored wool. Take out some piece of white-colored roving.
- Place it between the hat and the body on the back of the head.
- Felt it in place.

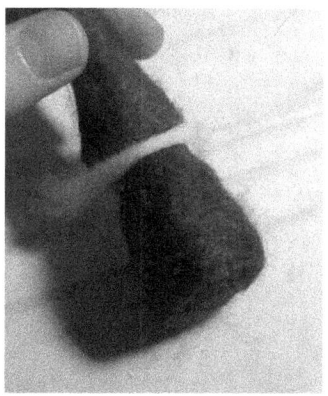

- Don't be too concerned with how you felt in the pieces around the face's front. In the next step, those will be covered up.

8. **Fixing the beard**

- Take out a strand of beard-colored roving (white).

- Fold it halfway so that it resembles the illustration below.

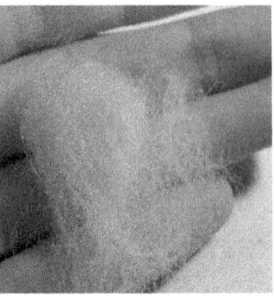

- Felt the upper area of the face and beneath the nose.

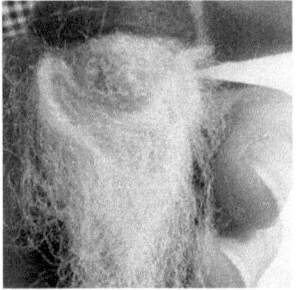

- Add another layer or two if necessary.
- Felt the beard into position with your needle. I like to curl it in the end, but it's entirely up to you.

You are done

Flower Brooch

Tools and Supplies

- Wool roving (dark tan) for the flower's petals
- 1 small rounded felt piece for the flower's center (1 inches)
- 1 large rounded felt piece for the flower's center (1 3/8 inches):
- 2 rounded felt piece for the flower's back (1 3/8 inches)
- Needle felting needle
- Felting pad or foam, or brush

Additional Tools and Supplies

- Thread for sewing the pin and button
- 1 button for the flower's center
- A brooch pin, 1 inches long
- Regular sewing needle
- Craft glue
- Scissors

Instructions

1. As shown below, needle felt five petals.

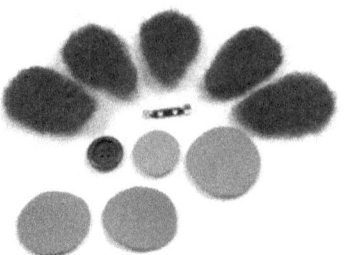

2. Place a rounded felt piece for the flower's back on top of the pad, brush or foam once you've completed the 5 petals. Then, as indicated in the illustration below, begin to arrange the petals of the flower around it, allowing them to overlap.

To hold each petal in place, stab the overlapping sections with the felting needle a few times.

3. Once you're satisfied with the petals arrangement, stab the flower's central area with the felting needle many times until the petals are firmly fastened to one another and to the rounded felt piece.

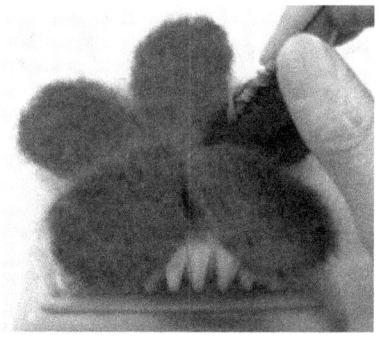

The felted circle on the backside of the flower would have a bit of wool fiber poking out of it, but don't bother. Later, we'll overlay it with another felt piece.

4. Thread a needle and prepare sewing the button on.

   In the middle of the flower's front side, lay the large and the mini felt pieces, along with the button at the upper most area.

   Sew the flower together with the button and the two felt pieces.

5. This is an optional step. Make incisions in the large felt piece to add texture to the flower if desired. (I trimmed the corners of every cut, as indicated in the final image of this project, making it pop the more)

6. Attach the brooch pin to the second rounded back piece and sew with a needle and thread.

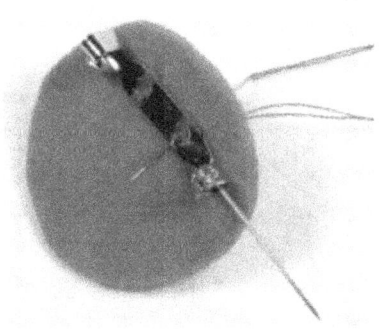

7. Glue the backside of the flower and gently place the second rounded piece over it.

8. You've completed your needle felted flower brooch. Now all you have to do is wait for the glue adhesive to dry.

Loop Bracelet

Tools and Supplies

- Colors of wool roving
- Needle felting needle in various sizes
- Needle felting pen (optional)
- Foam or pad

Additional Tools and Supplies

- Scissors
- Ruler

Instructions

1. Lay roving fibers that are 12-14 inches long (about 5 inches longer than required to wrap your wrist around) and double the breadth of your finished bracelet.

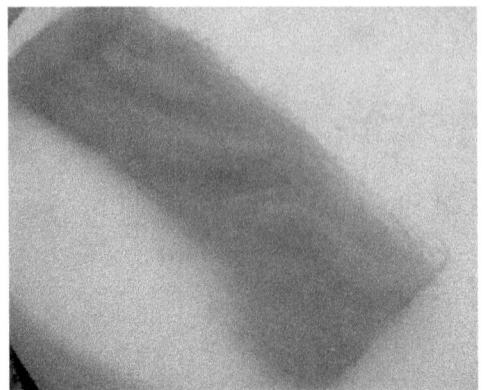

2. Next, set up small lengths of roving fibers over the preceding layer, 90 degrees from the direction of the preceding layer. Place the fibers evenly spaced and close together across the base of the bracelet.

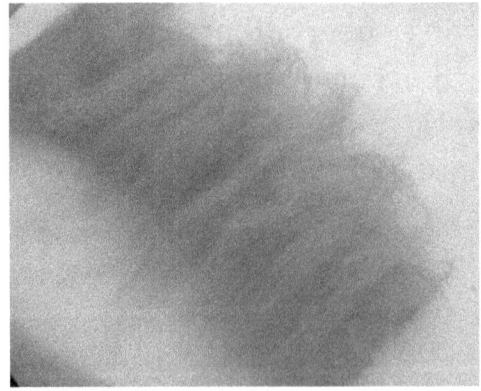

3. Diagonally cross opposing colors across the first two fiber layers. Note that, even if the fibers are laying thick right now, the needle felting process will condense all of the layers together considerably. Don't be scared to go for it when it comes to thickness. Continue layering fibers on this side until they reach a height of about 1 1/2 ".

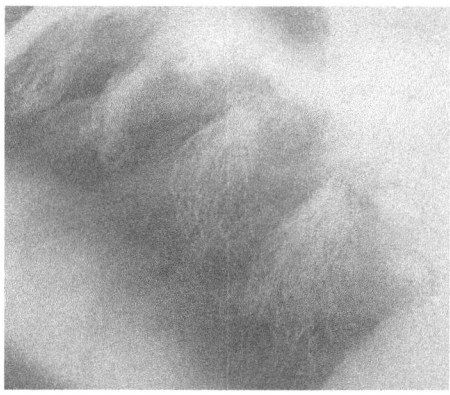

4. Start by poking a felting needle into the layers to fuse the wool fibers together. I like the use of a multi-needle pen for these larger levels.

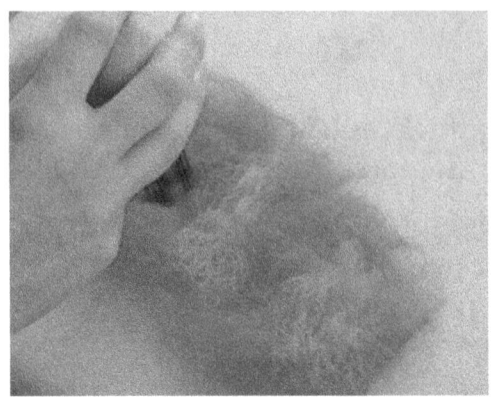

5. Lift the beginning-to-compact fibers out from the foam slowly and cautiously, starting at the corners and working to the middle. Remove the middle by stripping away from one side to another once the corners have been lifted. Turn it over to reveal the solid-colored side.

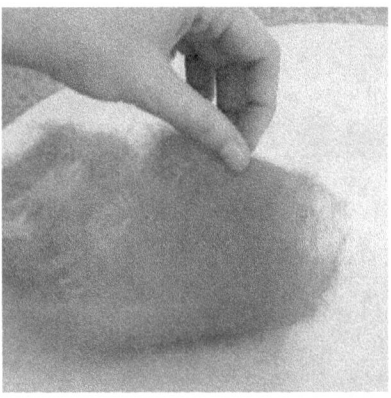

6. On this side, criss-cross additional opposing colored fibers, concentrating on areas of compacted fiber that appear thinner than others.

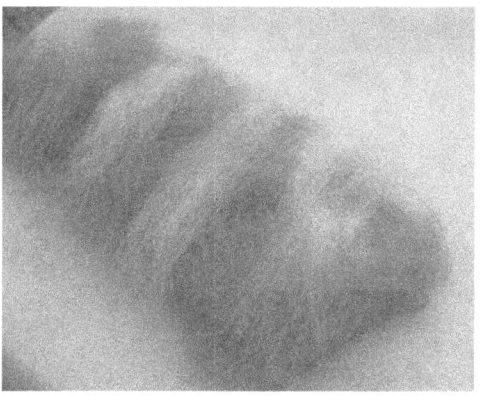

7. Continue needle-felting using the multi-needle pen, pressing the fibers together and occasionally lifting the rough bracelet formed from the foam.

    Flip the fibers frequently to ensure that they condense uniformly on both sides.

    If any sections appear to be lacking in fiber, add additional fiber and needle felt this section on both sides.

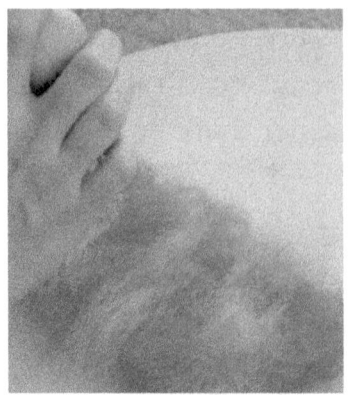

8. To blend and add visual appeal, pull and needle felt contrasting colors into one another. To maintain a smooth surface area, this step must be accomplished before the fibers have been totally mixed. When you've found the marble you like, needle felt across the top to firmly secure the colors, flipping frequently to lock in from both sides.

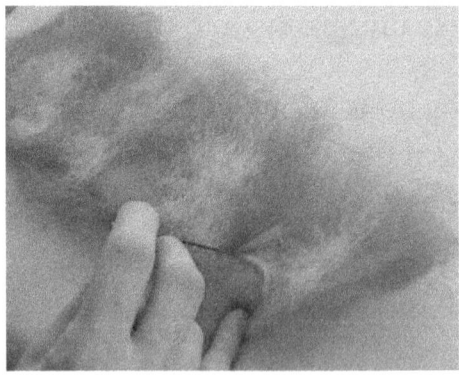

9. Start needling the bracelet's sides, beginning at the point of the width that's more narrow, with the upper side down. Start shaping using a coarse needle and work your way up to a finer gauge. Repeat on the opposite side.

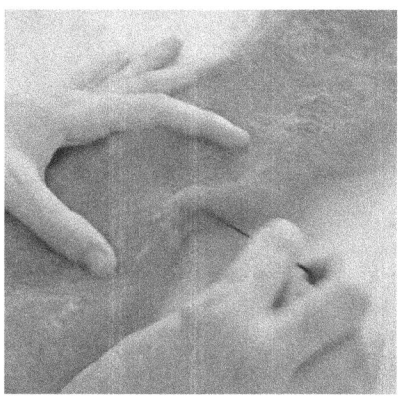

10. Upon completion, flip over the base of the bracelet and poke around the upper edge with the multi-needle pen. The exterior will be compacted and smoothed as a result. Repeat on the opposite side.

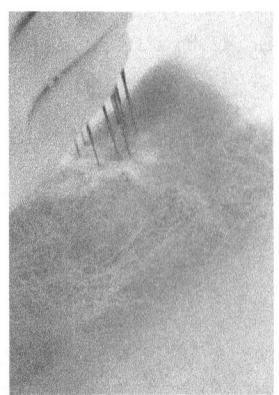

11. There are a few ways to complete this step, so I'll tell you which one I prefer. We're seeking to seal our freshly cut raw edge, and I prefer to do it by forcefully needling the end with my coarse needle. This forces a large number of fibers to pass through to the opposite side. Pull out the fibers with the needle's point near the cut edge until the end is somewhat whispy. Felt the whispy edges back across the cut end with a fine point needle. The cut end is smoothed and sealed as a result of this.

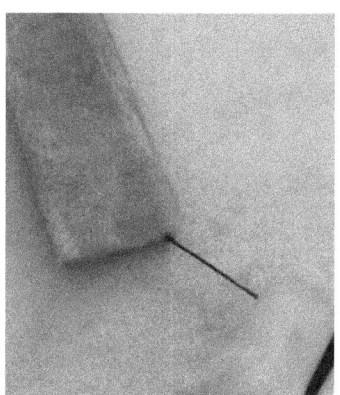

12. Measure 2 1/2 inches more than your wrist's length and use scissors to cut it off. Set aside the last piece to create the loop that ties the bracelet on your wrist.

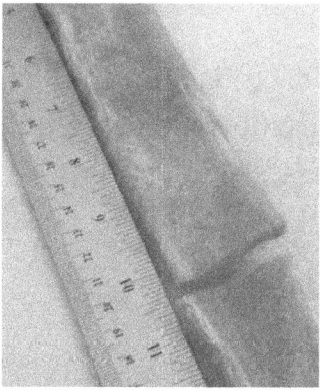

13. Curl very tiny pieces of roving in a contrasting color and felt into a design of your choice with a

small felting needle. Swirls, zigzags, and polka dots are examples of extremely simple, but yet appealing designs. Feel free to try new things. Needle felt the entire design a few times using the multi-needle pen to ensure it is tightly attached.

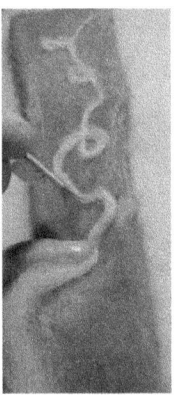

14. When the design is attached, part of the opposing color should show through on the opposite side. To attach these whispy opposing wool pieces to the back, felt over them.

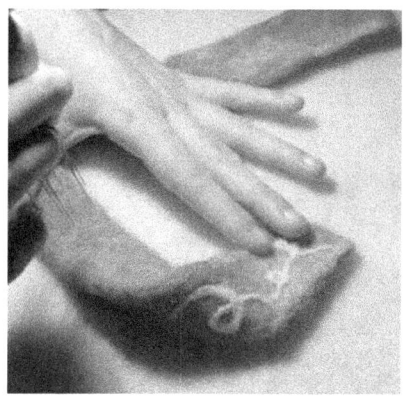

15. Twist the cut tail's remaining piece across one bracelet's end. I usually take advantage of this opportunity to conceal my less appealing side. Completely secure the loop to the bracelet's band with a coarse needle. Finish by using a small needle to secure any whispy parts.

Loop the free end of the fiber. To attach on your wrist, place across your hand and pull tight. The texture of the felt provides enough clinginess to keep the bracelet on your wrist.

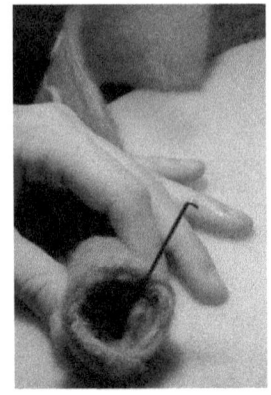 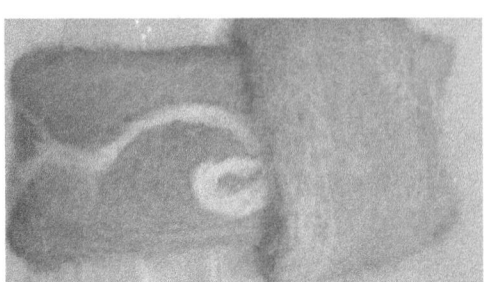

Pumpkin Earrings

Tools and Supplies

- Green and orange wool roving
- Needle felting needle
- Foam or pad

Additional Tools and Supplies

- Orange embroidery thread
- Earring hooks
- Embroidery needle
- Scissors

Instructions

1. Roll up a piece of orange wool that is roughly 20 x 2cm. To make a ball, roll it around in your hands.

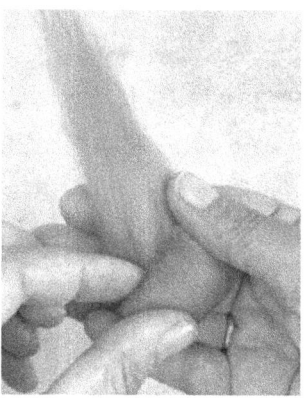

2. To begin felting the ball altogether, place it on a foam or pad, carefully pushing a felting needle in and out all around. Continue to push the needle until the ball is felted to a circumference of about 2cm.

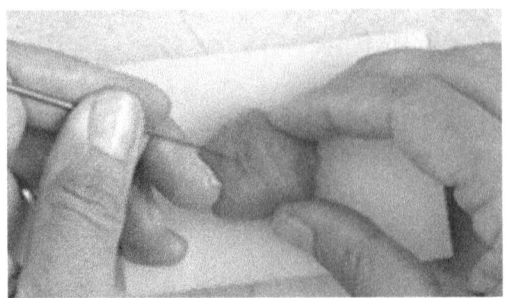

3. Take out two threads of reasonable length from an orange embroidery thread, threading them via an embroidery needle. Make a knot in one end and pull it up through the ball's center. Wrap the thread across the ball, then make it taut by pushing it up and through again.

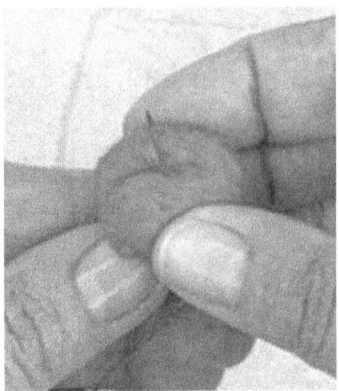

4. Wrap another five threads equally across the ball to make sections, repeating the process over the

entire ball. To make a pumpkin shape, pull each thread taut and slightly level the top and bottom of the ball.

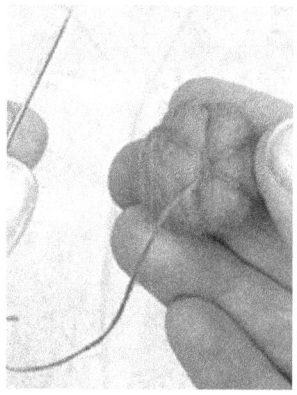

5. Lay the pumpkin on a foam or pad and use your needle to drive the threads deeper into the pumpkin while emphasizing the shape of the sections.

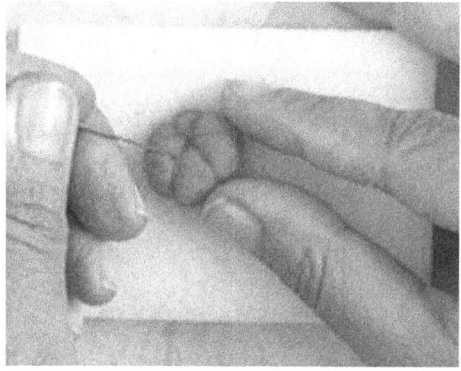

6. Take a little green wool piece and fold it in half, then in half again. Put it on a foam or pad, then make a stalk with your felting needle. Roll the stalk's top between your fingers once it has been felted.

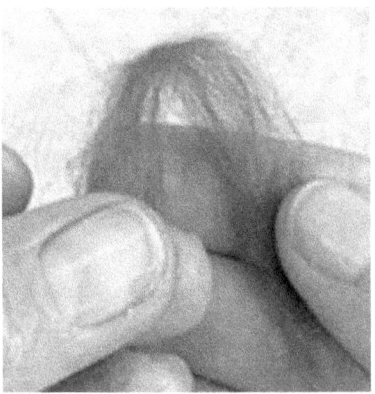

7. Attach the stalk to the pumpkin's top by felting the two pieces together, in and out around the base. Make a second pumpkin using the same method, then add earring hooks to the stalk's top.

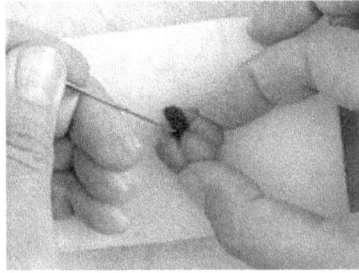

You are done!

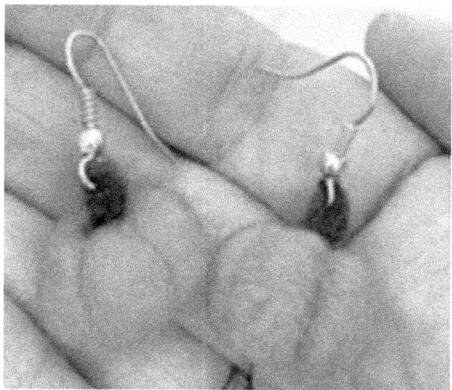

The End... Almost!

Hey! We've made it to the final chapter of this book, and I hope you've enjoyed it so far.

If you have not done so yet, I would be incredibly thankful if you could take just a minute to leave a quick review on Amazon

Reviews are not easy to come by, and as an independent author with a little marketing budget, I rely on you, my readers, to leave a short review on Amazon.

Even if it is just a sentence or two!

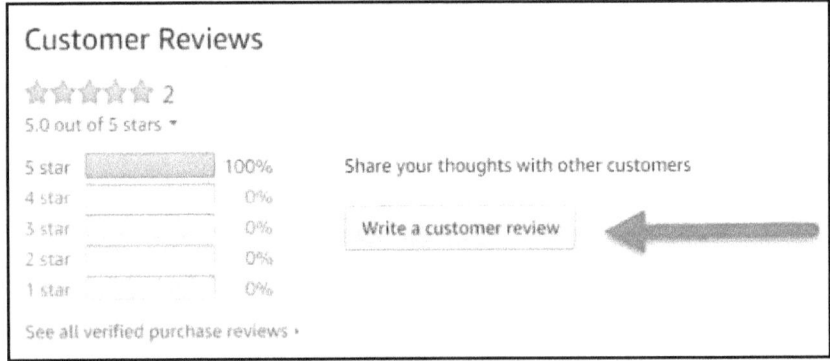

So if you really enjoyed this book, please...

>> Click here to leave a brief review on Amazon.

I truly appreciate your effort to leave your review, as it truly makes a huge difference.

Chapter 5

Fixing Common Needle Felting Problems

Help! My needle felting isn't coming out right! What's the matter?

Is your needle always breaking? Isn't the wool stiffening up? Is your felting uneven and rough on the surface?

Don't be anxious! Here's a rundown of the most frequent needle felting issues, along with some helpful solutions. Keep in mind we may have covered some of these under the tips and techniques chapter.

Wool Problems

Is it possible that my wool has a flaw? It does not appear to felt well enough

Some wools aren't suitable for felting, but if you got it as part of a kit, it should be alright – people have felt anything from bamboo to cat fur. The needle gauge is most likely the source of the problem. To test whether it makes a difference, try using a thicker (smaller number) needle. I'd suggest switching to a 32G triangular needle and see what happens.

My project is finished, however, my wool is still very fluffy. What's the best way to get a smooth finish?

If this is the situation, you should probably continue stabbing. I assess the firmness of my work by pressing my thumb into the middle of my palm (much to how you would test the doneness of a steak!). It's time to consider about achieving a smooth finish if my work is firm. Upon reaching this level of firmness, switch to a smaller needle and lessen your stab's depth to merely your needle's first set of notches. This should give your felt a beautiful smooth finish, but there will almost certainly be some stray fibers. Use your needle to tuck in as much as possible, but feel inclined to use scissors to cut some away.

I got some natural wool, and it stinks to high heaven. Is it possible to wash it to make it smell better?

Some people prefer the earthy, natural scent of wool, while others find it as a distraction from enjoying the felting process. It is probably not wise to wash the wool because you can end up felting it. Some people add lavender in their wool to improve the smell, either by making a cotton bag or by putting lavender soap bars in with it. This will also deter moths from snooping around your yummy wool stockpile.

Needle Problems

My needle appears to be broken. What exactly is going on?

If your wool isn't felting easily, you're probably using the incorrect needle - in this example, one that's too small for the work. To check if it makes a difference, consider using your thickest needle.

How can I tell which needle I'm using?

When I first started, I simply ordered a pack of felting needles from Amazon in the sizes S, M, and L. I tried looking up what type they could be and felting with them to figure it out, but I couldn't figure it out. They were all triangle needles since they had three sides, yet they all had the same amount of barbs and looked the same. So I had a number of inexpensive needles that broke quickly and performed the same thing.

All I am trying to imply is that it is worth getting needles from a company that informs you exactly what you are receiving, so you should already know what you are using. These are usually higher-quality needles that are color-coded, so you know what you're getting.

Problems With Felting Mat

What's up with my foam felting pad, which disintegrates as I felt?

Unfortunately, after a while of stabbing, foam felting pads tend to break up. It may be time to change your pad or upgrade to a new type, such as a wool pad. If you are set on foam, it's obviously time to invest in a new one. Look for the terms 'high density' in the product details to see if the item will last longer.

What is the best way to clean my felting mat?

Wool sticking to the felting mat is one of the minor inconveniences of needle felting, but it's quite simple to fix. In most cases, simply picking the wool off your pad will suffice; however, the following ways will also suffice:

- Wrap adhesive tape over your hand (adhesive side out) and pat the pad to ensure that the wool fibers adhere to the tape.
- Use a clothes brush, like the type you'd use to get the fluff out of a garment.

I've discovered that when you attempt to pull the wool fibers out of a foam pad, the soft foam comes off with it. This is an indication that it's time for your pad to be changed.

Other General Mistakes

Working too deeply when felting

Even now, I'm bad at doing this. I typically put the needle in too deep because I'm so eager to get everything felt down as soon as possible. This is a typical mistake, particularly among beginners. Because the needles have barbs, you can just felt into the barb's depths.

You don't need to felt too deeply; a simple in/out movement to your barb's depth will suffice. I understand why some people disagree with this. Felting too deeply could cause your needle to come off at the other side of your piece and stick to the pad, or if you felt much too deeply, you could actually fracture the needle by hitting it on the base below.

Not making use of a pad

If you don't use a support pad, you're doing yourself a disservice.

Some people choose to hold their felting instead of using a pad, foam, or brush. This indicates that your felting lacks a frame from which to operate, implying that your piece has not been properly felted. Because you don't have as much control, you're more likely to get injured or break your needle.

Attempting to merge two completed pieces of work

If you are working on a project that demands parts to be connected together, one of the mistakes you can do is to finish each part before attempting to join them. What you should do is to leave the join area of the piece unfinished. Leave a few loose fibers to needle felt into the next piece. This makes it easier to join the felting together. Also, you don't want your piece to be totally completed; otherwise, joining pieces together would be more difficult, and the joint will not hold as well, resulting in a weak joint.

Working with too much or too little wool

Many people work with far too much wool. My mistake was that I always used far too little and took a long time to felt up. So consider what you're doing and adjust the amounts properly, whether it is too much or too little felt. Too much felt might be difficult to felt down, causing your work to seem lumpy and ruined. You also don't want to remove the felt. While some people remove the felt to re-create the pieces, it's better to avoid this when you're first starting out because adding wool is easier than removing it.

Conclusion

We've reached the conclusion of this excellent read. If you've made it this far in the book, I congratulate you; you're the type of person who succeeds.

This book has given you thorough information on needle felting as well as step-by-step guidance on how to do needle felting. You've also learned how to make about 10 different projects that range from Owls to Gnome, Flower Brooch, and Loop Bracelet, among many others.

You can make your projects as simple or as complicated as you want, but I advise you to start with simple projects as a beginner and get the hang of it before moving onto complex projects, so you don't get overwhelmed.

Also, while felting, take the appropriate safety precautions. Always utilize a felting foam, pad, or brush and keep an eye on your movements, proceeding with caution. Please do not hurt yourself. As you improve, you can adjust your speed accordingly.

It is an honor for me to accompany you on this adventure, and I believe in you wholeheartedly.

So, get your felting needles and start making beautiful crafts RIGHT AWAY!

www.ingramcontent.com/pod-product-compliance
Lightning Source LLC
Chambersburg PA
CBHW071420070526
44578CB00003B/628